This
Book
Belongs
To _____

PSALMS And PROVERBS

Written by Alice Joyce Davidson
Illustrated by Victoria Marshall

Text copyright © 1984 by Alice Joyce Davidson
Art copyright © 1984 by The C.R. Gibson Company
Published by The C.R. Gibson Company
Norwalk, Connecticut 06856
Printed in Spain by Artes Graficas Toledo S.A.
All rights reserved
ISBN 0-8378-5069-X
D. L. TO: 1207 -1985

The C.R. Gibson Company, Norwalk, Connecticut 06856

Alice went to Bible School
To learn of God's great ways.

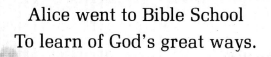

She read the Psalms and Proverbs
For advice and words of praise.

Alice thought of all she learned
And knew it would be fun

To make up rhymes and songs of praise
To share with everyone.

Jov cometh in the morning.

Psalms 30:5

The sun is smiling at me.
Joy is in the air!
A brand new day has started.
God's love is everywhere.

This is the day which the Lord hath made;
we will rejoice and be glad in it.

Psalms 118:24

Every second,
  every minute,
Every day
  has glad things in it.
For every day
  the whole year through
Was made by God
  for me and you.

I will praise thee;
for I am fearfully and wonderfully made.

Psalms 139:14

God made me and I can talk,
And I can sing, and pray;
I can touch, and smell, and hear,
And see new joys each day;
For God gave me a mind, and heart—
A soul that knows His way.

So teach us to number our days,
that we may apply our hearts unto wisdom.

Psalms 90:12

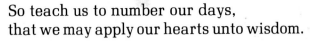

There's so much, God,
       to see, to hear,
There's so much, God, to know,
Please stay beside me
       day by day
And help me learn and grow!

The desire accomplished is sweet to the soul.

Proverbs 13:19

How nice it is to have a dream—
A special goal to do.
How sweet it is when goals are met
And happy dreams come true!

Be thou diligent to know the state of thy flocks.

Proverbs 27:23

Kitty cats to cuddle,
Puppy dogs to run—
Having pets to care for
Is a special kind of fun!

He that walketh with wise men shall be wise.

Proverbs 13:20

Pick somebody wiser
Whom you can walk beside
And you'll see a whole lot better
As your eyes will open wide.
Pick somebody wiser
Whom you can listen to
And you'll be a whole lot smarter
In everything you do.

Even a child is known by his doings,
whether his work be pure,
and whether it be right.

Proverbs 20:11

I've got a lot to learn yet,
    but I know one thing for sure—
I feel good when I do my best
    and when my heart is pure.

Commit thy works unto the Lord,
and thy thoughts shall be established.

Proverbs 16:3

If what you do is for the Lord,
Then you will have a sweet reward . . .
For all who follow in His way
Are blessed with peace and joy each day.

Create in me a clean heart, O God;
and renew a right spirit within me.

Psalms 51:10

Please help me, God, be better,
I'd like that if You would,
Because I know You're happier
When I'm especially good.

Thou hast made summer and winter.

Psalms 74:17

Summer, winter, spring and fall
Are filled with wonders through and through;
For every season, one and all,
Was made by God who made us, too.

Blessed be the Lord who daily
loadeth us with benefits.

Psalms 68:19

In front of me,
  behind me,
    above me, and around me,
Everywhere I go,
  I know
    God's loving gifts surround me!

Trust in the Lord with all thine heart;
and lean not unto thine own understanding.

Proverbs 3:5

Sometimes it's hard to understand
Why this or that is so,
But trust the Lord—He'll answer
When the time is right to know.

Oh, Lord, attend unto my cry,
give ear unto my prayer.

Psalms 17:1

When I'm feeling troubled
And my heart is filled with care,
I gather up my troubles
And go to God in prayer.
And when I'm feeling good again
And joy is everywhere,
I pay God a little visit
With a happy thank-you prayer.

A man's heart deviseth his way:
but the Lord directeth his steps.

Proverbs 16:9

I can go from there to here,
Or go from here to there,
And everywhere I go, God IS—
For God is everywhere!

I will fear no evil:
for thou art with me.

Psalms 23:4

When I'm afraid, I close my eyes
And say a prayer . . . and then
I feel God watching over me
And I'm okay again!

Enter not into the path of the wicked,
and go not in the way of evil men.

Proverbs 4:14

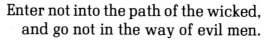

There's a two-letter word
That's easily heard
When temptation comes your way . . .

If you think you may stray
Just remember to say
That two-letter word—
NO!

The Lord is gracious, and full of compassion;
slow to anger, and of great mercy.

Psalms 145:8

Sometimes when I'm bad,
It makes me quite sad,
But I know that the good Lord above
Forgives what I do,
and blesses me, too,
With His special and wonderful love!

A soft answer turneth away wrath.

Proverbs 15:1

When someone talks with anger,
Don't let it get you down . . .
Answer anger with a smile
And you'll chase away a frown!

Pleasant words are as an honeycomb,
sweet to the soul,
and health to the bones.

Proverbs 16:24

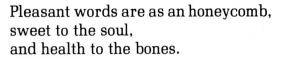

Give someone an extra lift
With pleasant words of praise
For compliments are special gifts
That add such joy to days.

A merry heart maketh a cheerful countenance.

Proverbs 15:13

A great big smile
Is so worthwhile,
It brightens up a day
For sad folks, mad folks,
Already glad folks—
And all who come your way!

The desire of a man is his kindness.

Proverbs 19:22

Caring, sharing, being kind—
That's what life's about . . .
God fills our hearts with lots of love
Which we, in turn, give out.

Behold, how good and how pleasant it is
for brethren to dwell together in unity!

Psalms 133:1

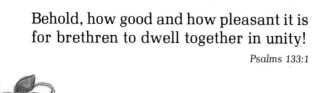

I've small friends, tall friends,
light friends, dark friends,
friends of every kind . . .
And everywhere I go
I know new friends
are nice to find!

A friend loveth at all times.

Proverbs 17:17

Who's with me
When I'm up or down?
Who cheers me
When I wear a frown?
Who has a helping hand
To lend?
MY FRIEND!

A man that hath friends
must shew himself friendly.

Proverbs 18:24

Lend a hand, and give an ear,
Share a dream or plan—
To have a friend, just be a friend
In every way you can.

To the counsellors of peace is joy.

Proverbs 12:20

Let's join our hands and work for good,
And work for peace and brotherhood;
Let's understand each other's ways
And help bring peaceful, happy days.

It is a good thing
to give thanks unto the Lord.

Psalms 92:1

Thank You, God, for loving parents,
Thank You, God, for food to eat.
Thank You, God, for all Your seasons,
For winter's snow, for summer's heat.
Thank You, God, for glowing rainbows,
Thank You, God, for birds that sing.
Thank You, God, for all Your wonders,
Thank You, God, for everything!

Serve the Lord with gladness:
come before his presence with singing.

Psalms 100:2

I have a song of thanks to sing
For all the happy things You bring,
Thank You, Lord, for everything.
I thank You, Lord, Amen!

I feel a song of praise is due
For all the gifts we get from You,
For all the love You give us, too,
I love You, Lord, Amen!

The Lord is my shepherd; I shall not want.

Psalms 23:1

He is my shepherd,
I am His lamb,
The closer to God,
the happier I am!